To Celebrate

Date

THANK YOU FOR COMING.

Let's celebrate!

Guest Name

Wishes & Messages

Email/Phone

Guest Name

Wishes & Messages

EMAIL/PHONE

Guest Name

Wishes & Messages

Email/Phone

Guest Name
Wishes & Messages
Email/Phone

Guest Name

Wishes & Messages

Email/Phone

Guest Name

Wishes & Messages

Email/Phone

Guest Name
Wishes & Messages
Email/Phone

Guest Name

Wishes & Messages

EMAIL/PHONE

Guest Name
Wishes & Messages
Email/Phone

Guest Name
Wishes & Messages
Email/Phone

Guest Name

Wishes & Messages

Email/Phone

Guest Name

____

Wishes & Messages

____

____

____

____

____

____
Email/Phone

Guest Name
____

Wishes & Messages

____
____
____
____
____
____
Email/Phone

Guest Name

Wishes & Messages

Email/Phone

Guest Name

Wishes & Messages

Email/Phone

Guest Name
Wishes & Messages
Email/Phone

Guest Name

Wishes & Messages

Email/Phone

Guest Name

Wishes & Messages

EMAIL/PHONE

Guest Name
Wishes & Messages
Email/Phone

Guest Name
Wishes & Messages
Email/Phone

Guest Name

Wishes & Messages

Email/Phone

Guest Name

Wishes & Messages

Email/Phone

Guest Name

Wishes & Messages

Email/Phone

Guest Name
Wishes & Messages
Email/Phone

Guest Name

Wishes & Messages

Email/Phone

Guest Name

____

Wishes & Messages

____

____

____

____

____

Email/Phone _______________________________________

Guest Name

Wishes & Messages

Email/Phone

Guest Name
Wishes & Messages
EMAIL/PHONE

Guest Name

Wishes & Messages

Email/Phone

Guest Name

Wishes & Messages

Email/Phone

Guest Name

Wishes & Messages

EMAIL/PHONE

Guest Name

Wishes & Messages

Email/Phone

Guest Name

Wishes & Messages

Email/Phone

Guest Name

Wishes & Messages

Email/Phone

Guest Name

Wishes & Messages

Email/Phone

Guest Name
Wishes & Messages
EMAIL/PHONE

Guest Name

Wishes & Messages

Email/Phone

Guest Name

Wishes & Messages

EMAIL/PHONE

Guest Name

Wishes & Messages

Email/Phone

Guest Name
Wishes & Messages
EMAIL/PHONE

Guest Name

Wishes & Messages

EMAIL/PHONE

Guest Name

Wishes & Messages

EMAIL/PHONE

Guest Name

Wishes & Messages

Email/Phone

Guest Name

Wishes & Messages

E
Email/Phone

Guest Name

Wishes & Messages

Email/Phone

Guest Name

Wishes & Messages

Email/Phone

Guest Name

Wishes & Messages

Email/Phone

Guest Name

Wishes & Messages

Email/Phone

Guest Name

____

Wishes & Messages

____

____

____

____

____

____

Email/Phone

Guest Name

Wishes & Messages

Email/Phone

Guest Name
Wishes & Messages
Email/Phone

Guest Name

Wishes & Messages

EMAIL/PHONE

Guest Name

Wishes & Messages

Email/Phone

Guest Name

Wishes & Messages

Email/Phone

Guest Name

____

Wishes & Messages

____

____

____

____

____

Email/Phone

Guest Name

Wishes & Messages

EMAIL/PHONE

Guest Name

Wishes & Messages

Email/Phone

Guest Name

Wishes & Messages

Email/Phone

Guest Name

Wishes & Messages

Email/Phone

Guest Name
Wishes & Messages
Email/Phone

Guest Name

Wishes & Messages

Email/Phone

Guest Name
Wishes & Messages
Email/Phone

Guest Name
Wishes & Messages
Email/Phone

Guest Name

Wishes & Messages

EMAIL/PHONE

Guest Name
Wishes & Messages
Email/Phone

Guest Name

Wishes & Messages

EMAIL/PHONE

Guest Name

Wishes & Messages

Email/Phone

Guest Name
Wishes & Messages
Email/Phone

Guest Name

____

Wishes & Messages

____

____

____

____

____

EMAIL/PHONE
____

Guest Name

Wishes & Messages

Email/Phone

Guest Name
Wishes & Messages
Email/Phone

Guest Name

Wishes & Messages

E
Email/Phone

Guest Name

Wishes & Messages

Email/Phone

Guest Name

Wishes & Messages

Email/Phone

Guest Name

Wishes & Messages

Email/Phone

Guest Name
Wishes & Messages
Email/Phone

Guest Name

Wishes & Messages

Email/Phone

Guest Name
Wishes & Messages
EMAIL/PHONE

Guest Name

Wishes & Messages

Email/Phone

Guest Name

Wishes & Messages

EMAIL/PHONE

Guest Name
Wishes & Messages
Email/Phone

Guest Name

Wishes & Messages

Email/Phone

Guest Name

Wishes & Messages

Email/Phone

Guest Name

Wishes & Messages

E
Email/Phone

Guest Name
Wishes & Messages
Email/Phone

Guest Name

Wishes & Messages

Email/Phone

Guest Name

Wishes & Messages

Email/Phone

Guest Name

Wishes & Messages

Email/Phone

Guest Name

Wishes & Messages

Email/Phone

Guest Name
Wishes & Messages
Email/Phone

Guest Name

Wishes & Messages

Email/Phone

Guest Name
Wishes & Messages
Email/Phone

Guest Name

Wishes & Messages

Email/Phone

Guest Name

Wishes & Messages

Email/Phone

Guest Name

Wishes & Messages

Email/Phone

Guest Name

Wishes & Messages

EMAIL/PHONE

Guest Name
Wishes & Messages
Email/Phone

Guest Name
Wishes & Messages
EMAIL/PHONE

Guest Name

Wishes & Messages

EMAIL/PHONE

Guest Name

Wishes & Messages

EMAIL/PHONE

Guest Name
Wishes & Messages
Email/Phone

Guest Name

Wishes & Messages

Email/Phone

Guest Name

Wishes & Messages

EMAIL/PHONE

Guest Name

Wishes & Messages

Email/Phone

Guest Name

Wishes & Messages

E
Email/Phone

NOTES & PHOTOS

NOTES & PHOTOS

NOTES & PHOTOS

NOTES & PHOTOS

GIFT LOG

Name /Email /Phone	Gift

GIFT LOG

Name / Email / Phone
Gift

GIFT LOG

Name /Email /Phone | Gift

GIFT LOG

Name / Email / Phone **Gift**

GIFT LOG

Name / Email / Phone	Gift

GIFT LOG

Name /Email /Phone	Gift

GIFT LOG

Name / Email / Phone	Gift